# DEDICATION

# DEDICATION

## *by Ruth Alford Read*

JOHN F. BLAIR, Publisher
Winston-Salem, North Carolina

# Contents

# DEDICATION

No . . .
it's an impossible task.

To Dad
because he was
(and is)
my big masculine ideal . . .

                  To Mama

just because . . .

                  Guy, John, Ben,

Beck, Weesie, Gay . . .

Charlie Coral Laura Michelle
Shari
Don Annette

                  Donna

Pagliacci?

you . . .or you . . .or
good old what's-his-name?

                  youoryouoryou

1 2 3 4 5
a b c d e f g
eeny meeny miney mo . . .

what about those who might still appear?

## DEDICATION

To: _____

(Please fill in the blank.)

# LINES TO MY MOTHER

When I think of you
all the memories that are mine
become diamonds and sapphires . . .

                    undimmed by time

and untarnished.

I remember the smell of yeast bread
and the lilac by the garage door.
I remember the sound of your voice

                    singing . . .
                    giggling, sometimes . . .
                    calling me in from play.

I remember the old, overworked sewing machine
(treadle type!)
which was my path to learning
and the patience and willingness
that walked hand-in-hand
with your lessons to me.

I remember
saying my nightly,

                    little-girl

prayers at your knee.

When I think of you
my wish is to be like you
so that my daughter
will know what a mother is . . .

3

so that *her* daughter will know.

This is my greatest tribute to you.

When I think of you
it is with humble gratitude

and fierce pride . . .

it begins in tenderness
and ends

in prayer.

# SONG OF EASTER
## (To My Dad)

The Lord is risen!

It begins as the slightest stirring . . .
the faintest motion

                    somewhere deep within me.

It is the movement of an unborn child
barely making its presence known.

                    It is a whisper.

Some enchanting cherub whispers inside me:

                    Psst! The Lord is risen!

It is the voice of a four-year-old
whispering

                    I love you, Mommy.

Too precious to be shared . . .
too intimate to be said aloud.

                    The Lord is risen!

The words are reaffirmed as I scan my garden
and see the hand of God
on the daffodils . . .

on the tulips and lilacs
and on each budding leaf

and my ear is attuned
to the sound of Heaven

                in the robin's first song.

The Lord is risen!

It becomes a march . . .

                jubilant, exultant, triumphant!

The Lord is risen!
The Lord is risen!
The Lord is risen!

It grows and swells within me
until it cannot be contained.

It becomes a shout . . .

a silent screaming inside my soul
so magnificent in its magnitude
that it cries for release . . .

so prolifically profound
that it must
burst forth in a wild cacophony of sound
that mingles and blends with all the voices of Nature.

The Lord is risen!

                I sing!

I sing . . .and I . . .

even I

can join the angels in the song of the centuries . . .
in the anthem of the ages:

The Lord is risen!

# PSALM

Blessed art thou, O Lord
for tolerating the likes of a man . . .
woman . . .

                        me . . .

for allowing us to be headstrong
even though we faint . . .
unyielding
even though we cry for tenderness . . .
stubborn
even though we ask for understanding.

Blessed art thou, O God
for granting the privilege

                        of anger

even though we seek peace . . .
of jealousy
even though we demand love . . .
of envy
even though we recognize our own inadequacies.

Blessed art thou, O Lord
for the beauty

                        of truth

even though we blaspheme . . .
of bravery
even though we are cowards . . .

of joy
even though we mourn.

Blessed art thou,
O Lord!

## TO MY PARENTS
### On July 25, 1965

Sixty-one years ago
on this date
two people stood before a minister
and said some words.

They were very special words,
but then,
these were very special people.

They knew that these words
would build a marriage.

                              And so,

for more than half a century
they worked at giving the words
new depth
and greater meaning . . .
realizing that each additional year
added a luster all its own.

                          As a result,

the marriage that was consummated
so long ago
will remain unbroken
and undestroyed

as long as there is a child,
a grandchild,
or a great-grandchild

who can look back on it

in their memory
and who will be able
to draw strength

from its existence.

                              Thank you

for a legacy
far greater than riches.

# SPLASHDOWN—APOLLO 15

I saw the drogue chute
one split instant
before the TV announcer said:

there it is!

I watched it grow bigger
and then disappear
into the enveloping purity
of one gigantic cloud.

When it emerged,
the cloud had inexplicably
taken on the shape of a face . . .

hair, nose, mouth, eyebrows . . .

eyes looking down
at the precious cargo
it had just harbored.

I wondered
how many people
saw the face of God today.

# TO DEATH

I've been in your presence before
but never so close . . .
never so aware . . .

I watch for things you do
(as if I needed a reminder)

small things
that only love-filled eyes could see.

And I wish you away.

Be a dream . . .

please . . .

be a dream.

Don't come any nearer
not yet
I'm not ready for you again.

You've lost your fascination for me
and have filled me with fear
and anxiety

and rebellion

and I know
that instead of being a dream
you are

the only truth.

13

# ROADMAPS

What magnificent/malevolent
    demon
        god
devises the roadmap of life . . .

giving clarion directions

    *turn left*
    *proceed to first intersection*
    *stop, look, and listen*
    *do not pass ''go''*

willing you to obey
because you're afraid of the dark
and your own weaknesses

    *the bogey man will get you*

leading you
willingly and will-lessly
until you realize

there were no directions
no instructions . . .

you got here by yourself

    *with a little help from your friends*

into this maze

    *through the looking glass*
    *we see through a glass darkly . . .*

HELP!

                Hear the cry!

Who hears the cry?
Not the demon/god.

                After rubbing his golden belly .

with satisfied glee
he goes back to contemplating his navel

before he begins plotting another roadmap.

# TO CORAL ON HER BIRTHDAY

A hand held yours
when you made your first, tentative

       baby-step

out of the world of fantasy
and into the world of reality

and an unseen presence
was your companion
with each giant-step

       of decision.

Your tears could not fall
from my eyes
nor could your kiss
come from my lips.

But how can I say
I have watched you grow?

To have watched
would indicate my own static existence
and would have resulted
in your leaving me behind.

The passage of time
leaves all mortals in its wake . . .
touching everyone . . .

allowing no escape

                or shelter . . .

offering no refuge
except love.

# TO MAMA

Poor old lady
sitting by the window
marking time . . .
waiting for the Great Conqueror . . .

with nothing to live for
except the children
who can give you so little time
in return for all the time
you've given them.

                    Sure,

they have it made . . .
thanks to you.

(Are your investments
paying enough dividends?)

But you're still a smart old cookie
and your perception hasn't dimmed
with age.

You know

                    (don't you?)

that the pretty packages
and the extra money
are the only ways they have to say:

                    Thanks, Mom.

18

Poor old lady
sitting by the window . . .
I see your tired hands
and your pale blue eyes
and I wonder what those eyes see
that I'm not privileged to see.

Sit there, and wait . . .
rest your tired hands
and let your eyelids flutter
over all of yesterday's memories . . .

let the blue eyes gaze
over the fields
trying to penetrate the curtain of tomorrow

and forever.

You look so right there . . .
you belong there so much
that every time I drive around the house
I shall see you there

blowing me that last kiss.

# PRAYER

O Lord
hear my prayer . . .

whatever it is.

There is so much to pray for
and about . . .
but when I begin with thanksgiving
my mind wanders
to what's next . . .

and if I go to my help-wanted list
I return to something
I forgot to be thankful for.

When I ask Your blessings on others,
it eventually, inevitably becomes
God Bless Me . . .

and I feel I should begin anew
and try a little harder
to leave me out of it.

I'm not given to oratory . . .
even conversation lags at times . . .
but when I hear
such beautiful words
falling effortlessly from other tongues

I wonder why my own attempts
always begin and end with

O Lord
hear my prayer . . .

whatever it is.

# DEDICATION II

If you have been
important enough
to warrant a

D E D I C A T I O N

you have shared more
of me
than could possibly fit

on a flyleaf.

# THE VOICE

(Coral, at age 12, wrote me the following note:
"Sometime in a poem try to discribe [sic] how
Christ's voice might sound if we could hear him
speak.")

It was just a voice . . .
deep, masculine,
resonant.

It could have belonged to any man.

It was not the voice
of a god . . .

it was only

man's voice speaking with God's authority.

It spoke not of politics
but in parables . . .
simple words with simple meanings.

It spoke not in oration
but in obedience.

It spoke not of kings
but of The Kingdom.

It spoke not of lust
but of love.

It spoke

to the many
and to the few.
It spoke to the wayfarer
and the wanderer

and to all who had ears to hear
and hearts to receive.

It was just a voice . . .

Be still, my child.
If you are very quiet

you can hear it still.

# REINCARNATION

I must have known you
in some other life
because recognition was instantaneous

                              and complete.

I must have loved you before this
because the experience of

you

is not strange
but rather a reminiscence
of another time and place

when I was a different me . . .
totally capable of love
and minus the questions and doubts
I now allow.

We could not have reached this point
in so short a time
if this path had not been traveled before . . .

Who were you then?
and who was I?

                              . . . and how were we?

If all the teachings are true
and we actually do reach a higher plateau . . .
an ascendant level of understanding
and peace . . .

then our foreyears must have been spent
in a particular kind of hell.

But if you believe I will come to you again
  . . . or you to me . . .
in some afterlife of which we have no knowledge . . .

we should start now
to prepare the way

                              for that unbelievable Eden.

# OUR SPECIAL BRAND

Somewhere
in the star-studded book of I Know

our page is written.

For a short time
during two separate eternities
we will be together

and I will share your youth
and all else that I wish to share

and you will have the comfort
of my understanding
and the wisdom of my experience

and we will share
our own special brand

                of love.

And then . . .
when we part
(a couple of millennia from now)
there will still be the flickering
bittersweet remains

of a solitary star.

# AWAKENING

I was a stranger
to myself.

I knew that somewhere
there was a separate entity
called me . . .

and I also knew
that the thing called me
was hiding from

me.

I was a brick wall
a barbed-wire fence
an oyster shell

but I knew that somewhere
in all the complexities
of that indefinable me

I was also a lute without strings
a canvas without paint
a song without words.

Then . . .
on a calm and comfortable Sunday evening
I watched your fingers
caress the strings of a guitar

and I was haunted by each note
and trembled with each chord.

I longed to be
the guitar . . .

to experience the response
awakened by your hands
and to sing the music
you wrote.

# FULLNESS

(1)

I am full of poetry today
(I am full today . . .
full and fulfilled.)

but most of my thoughts
are so beautifully private
that it's almost a sacrilege
to remove them from my brain.

So I keep them
written by you
on the forefront of my mind.

You know the thoughts . . .
you've loved me.

(2)

The car is full . . .
suitcases and paper bags
shoeboxes
all my painting gear

                              and you.

We share the morning fog
the first glimpse of the sun
the car radio
and complaints about other motorists.

It's only if I reach out my hand

to touch you
that I realize
the seat beside me

                    is empty.

And yet . . .
if I turn my head a certain way

                    . . . just so . . .

I can see my eyes in the mirror
and I know
your reflection is there

hiding somewhere
between my pupils and my sunglasses . . .

# EN ROUTE

My car leaves the main highway
and heads for the flatlands
of North Carolina.

The ribbon of concrete
stretches tirelessly on . . .
disappearing at the crest
of a rare hill
or simply vanishing
at the horizon . . .

leading from nowhere to nowhere.

I travel in a two-colored tunnel . . .
viridian on either side,
azure above.

Occasionally
the trees grow apart
and I glimpse corn and tobacco . . .

I've also seen cardinals
and thrushes
and other birds I don't know

and if I should see a deer
it would be my personal talisman.

A snake slithers onto the pavement
unaware of civilization
or approaching death

or anything since genesis
except the need to warm its belly.

I shudder
and speed onward.

# TIME, DISTANCE, AND POSSIBLE TRANSITION

So . . .
there are three elements to consider:

We must think of time, yes . . .
We must be ever-watchful
that we are always one step ahead . . .

that time does not approach unannounced
and jump the gun on us.

And distance . . .

what is distance
except the space that exists
between where you are
and where I am?

Can it be measured in miles, or light-years . . .
in hours
or forevers?

And as for my possible transition:
you cannot take a piece of gold
and make a brass ring . . .
just as a diamond
will always be a diamond

because it is real.

I mean:
you cannot change a thing of truth
into something counterfeit.

# PROLOGUE IS PROLOGUE TO EPILOGUE

Everything
is prologue.

Birth

to childhood

to adolescence

to maturity (we hope)
to age (middle and old)
to death.

The belief in Santa Claus
gives way to an unaccepting disbelief
in everything

which eventually becomes
a disbelieving acceptance

of everything.

Faith is transformed
into cynicism . . .
and souls lost in beauty and truth
become lost souls.

Somewhere along the way
we may learn to pray . . .

to God, to a god . . .
to a concept or an ideal
to something bigger and purer and brighter

because we recognize our need
admit our failures
seek assurance
cling to love
pray for peace.

### Prologue

seems to write itself
while we live through
each chapter and verse
all the time
writing our own epilogue.

# UNQUESTIONED ANSWERS

There are a few:

> Yes.
> No.
> Jesus loves me.
> I don't know.
> You know.

I love you.

# DEDICATION III

You know
who you are

       and why

and how
you have touched my life.

Why, then,
should there be
such joy

       and pride

in seeing your name in print?

Your name
has been inscribed
in a much more sacred place.

# TO LAURA

Beautiful
wood nymph . . .
all sun-kissed browns . . .

your home must be
in some enchanted forest
where elves and leprechauns
are your playmates

and the deer
is your best friend.

Your eyes are soft brown moss
and your smile
could illuminate
earth's darkest corner.

I hear your cascading laughter
and envision you
wearing veils of some diaphanous
gossamer materials

spun by a magic spider

flitting through the forest
pursued by a faun.

But wait . . .

where has my imagination
taken me?

My wood nymph

sleeps in her own bed . . .
brushes her teeth . . .
eats ice cream and spaghetti . . .
adores jeans and the telephone . . .

                    It's Laura . . .

she's 12 going on 35.

# TO MICHELLE

I have known you
since the moment of your birth
and I have spent these seven years
trying to get

                    to know you.

You are
a changeling . . .

                    fickle . . .

one moment you're just Shelley
but if I turn my back
or look away

Shelley disappears.

                    Instead . . .

I could be in the company of
Peter Pan
The Littlest Angel
Cinderella
any fairy-tale princess
or even
a Dresden doll.

I try to play your game
but just as I begin to feel secure
in playing Dopey
to your Snow White

                                you become Grandma Moses.

You don't believe
you've
        r
         e
          a
            l
             l
              y
                  fooled me, do you?

I've known all along
who you are:

Eve.

# POEMS . . .

are often better
left unwritten . . .

or at least
left unread by other eyes.

What is a poem, anyway,
except some random thought
momentarily enlarged
out of all proportion

and submitted to paper
as an offering . . .

                              a sacrifice

of the soul . . .

most often
torn
from some unexplored cranny
of the brain

with exquisite

                              torturous

pain.

Is it
one mind
communicating with itself

or simply
pen talking to paper?

Whichever it is,
it gives its own reasons
for not needing

other eyes.

(For Piney)

# CONTINUATION OF A CONVERSATION

In this today that is ours . . .
the one that leads
into an undetermined tomorrow . . .
there are no divisions of time . . .
no hours or o'clocks . . .
no dusks or dawns . . .

only the urgent intensity

                                    of now.

It will remain today
as long as you are here.

And when that tomorrow arrives
and your physical presence is gone
and leaves a void in my life . . .

when time is again measured
and the clock hands continue
in their monotonous circle . . .
and all my predestined days
are again divided
into mornings and midnights . . .

then I will include you
in my other yesterdays
and place your memory
somewhere between birth and death.

And . . . in the after-day . . .
that period that follows all tomorrows . . .

when I have

                    finally

stopped loving you
and when time stands still for all of us . . .

there should be some perpetual sign . . .
some rainbow arc of varied hues
leaving the earth
ascending
falling gently and beautifully
to earth again . . .

commemorating the day that was ours.

(For Alan)

# TO CHRIS

You're such an impossible kid . . .

Every normal,
red-blooded,
All-American
(almost) 12-year-old boy

should be
(according to all standards)
totally obnoxious.

                    Not to be

is to be unfaithful
to God and church
Mom and apple pie

not to mention dear old Dad.

                    But you . . .

blue eyes and freckled nose
blond tousled hair
braces

sashaying right up to me
in church
and

                    HUGGING ME!

I had to stand on tiptoe
to kiss the top of your head . . .

even though I had grown
ten feet tall.

I love you,
Christopher Monte King,
boy/child/man.

# LET ME HELP

Let me help
in whatever ways
and at whatever times
you decide you need me.

The decision is yours . . .

I could not know when or how
nor could I presume constancy

or duration.

(Did you ever wonder

how the third string quarterback
feels when he is suddenly
and unexpectedly
called in for action?)

But you must let me help
if only because
I want it so much . . .

at least,

let me think I help.

I need that
in order to maintain
the feeling of importance

to myself.

(For Alan)

# DEDICATION IV

These are for you . . .

words.

Common, ordinary, unpolished,
everyday sounds . . .

words of little meaning
and less consequence . . .

syllables and synonyms
verbs and adverbs

pronouns and prepositions.

It is such an unworthy offering . . .
so terribly unfitting . . .
so very inadequate.

It is all

I have to give.

You see,

the gods could not compose a new language
or a special set of words
for you and me.

Instead,

they endowed the same old sounds
with a very special meaning.

# TODAY

I am filled
with the magical self-assurance
that comes only from:

somebody loves me.

If you have any doubts,
look at my eyes

and watch the way I walk.

# SILENT SOUNDS

Have you ever
heard a smile?

                              It sounds

just like fingertips.

They both seem to go:

mmmmm
        mmmmm
                mmmmm.


# DAYS

. . . automatically
shorten themselves
until they are no longer
days.

                              This one

gets longer
and longer . . .

Where are you?

51

# STRAWBERRIES AND SHAVING CREAM

It's a crazy
beautiful
mixed-up
wonderful world

when fresh strawberries
on my cereal
are the manifestation

                              of your love.

And when deep-born chuckles
keep playing games
with my insides
because you said:

I love you, too,
but I'm shaving.

You will be with me all day . . .
written on my smile
and mirrored in my eyes.

# ARGUMENTS

. . . foreign to reason . . .
emotions with self-inflicted wounds . . .
voices raised in a crescendo

                              of vanity.

Half-glances, through eyes full of shadows
or full-face stares
fraught with questions.

Punishment . . .
*show me how much it hurts . . .*
Self-punishment
*so I can feel the pain myself . . .*
guess my mood
so I can see how effective the rules are . . .

or smug satisfaction
because I've fooled even you.

Is it a new game
we're playing . . .
or is it really
the end of an era?

                              Before we go

any further . . .
before I sink deeper into
this quicksand of doubt

I need whatever magic it is
that happens with your kiss.

53

# ADVENT

With infinite patience
and silent expectation
the earth turns itself
to accept another season . . .

                           like a woman

in love with her own destiny.

Our summer idyll is over
and we are left
to return to our former selves

only a little richer
(or wiser, perhaps)
but still needing help
from ourselves

                              . . . and others.

There will be no more
over-air-conditioned nights
when I absorbed warmth from your body
and used your arm as a pillow

and a shield.

Gin and tonic
goes out of season
when the weather
becomes cooler

and dry country roads

# AFTER GOODNIGHT

lay there for a while
after replacing the phone . . .

allowing your words
and the sound of your voice
to echo in my brain
and vibrate through my being . . .

with deliberate calm
I took them

(your words and the sound of your voice)

and spun a cocoon
of silken serenity
in which I slept.

leave a dust screen
that obscures
and eventually obliterates

all that is left behind.

## SUCH A STRANGE LAND

There is a never-never land . . .
I know
because I'm there.

I don't recall
a yellow brick road
or a Persian carpet . . .

I don't know how I got here . . .

but I know it's never-never land.
Everything tells me . . .
reminds me . . .

              warns me . . .

never before . . .

              never again.

You move so swiftly.

Changing everything you
swallowing all my todays
in your thirst for tomorrow

and I want
to slow you down
so I can savor these todays
while they are still warm

              w

and October sun.

I want you
to stand still . . .
not for too long . . .
just long enough
to allow other things

              to catch